THE TERRACOTTA ARMY

An Exploration of Xi'an's Pride and China's National Treasure

JAKE WHITEFIELD

Table of Contents

INTRODUCTION

Imagine a vast, silent army standing in perfect formation beneath the earth—thousands of soldiers, chariots, and horses frozen in time, waiting patiently to be discovered. For centuries, they lay in darkness, hidden from the world, their existence unknown until one fateful day in 1974 when farmers digging a well accidentally stumbled upon one of the most extraordinary archaeological finds in history. As the earth was pulled away, it revealed a massive subterranean army, each soldier meticulously crafted and positioned, as if poised to march into eternity. The discovery of the Terracotta Army was not only a historical revelation but also a glimpse into the mind of one of the most powerful and enigmatic rulers in Chinese history, Emperor Qin Shi Huang. This silent legion was a testament to his desire for eternal control and his relentless ambition to secure his place in both this life and the next.

Qin Shi Huang, the First Emperor of China, was a man of unparalleled vision and ruthlessness. His ambition knew no bounds; he not only unified China, establishing the foundation for a nation that still stands today, but he also embarked on a colossal project to ensure his rule would transcend death itself. The Terracotta Army, part of a much larger mausoleum complex that remains mostly unexcavated, was crafted to accompany him in the afterlife, protecting him as they had during his reign. Each of the thousands of figures is unique, embodying the emperor's command over an empire so vast and diverse. This ancient wonder offers more than just a glimpse of Qin Shi Huang's power—it reveals his belief in the continuity of authority beyond the grave, his determination to rule forever, and the lengths he would go to immortalize his empire, even in death. The discovery of the Terracotta Army has provided historians and archaeologists with a remarkable window into ancient China, giving us insight into not just the man who built it but the entire civilization he left behind.

Discovered in 1974 by farmers digging a well near Xi'an, China, the Terracotta Army stunned the world. What lay hidden beneath layers of earth for over two millennia was a sight of incredible grandeur: an army of life-sized warriors, meticulously crafted in clay, guarding the tomb of the emperor. These soldiers, with their intricate facial expressions and finely detailed armor, were not just statues but a reflection of the immense power and wealth of an emperor who believed in ruling the afterlife as he had in life.

Each figure was unique, representing the soldiers of his empire—from the infantrymen to archers and generals. But beyond their physical presence, they symbolized something greater: the might of an empire that once unified the warring states of China and the unyielding desire of one man to conquer eternity.

Historical Context

To truly grasp the significance of the Terracotta Army, one must step back into the world of the third century BCE. It was a time of war and chaos, where rival states battled for dominance in what would later become China. Qin Shi Huang, a young king of the state of Qin, rose to power with a singular vision: to unite the fractured lands under one banner. Through relentless military campaigns, cunning diplomacy, and brutal force, he achieved what many believed impossible.

In 221 BCE, Qin Shi Huang declared himself the First Emperor of China, the ruler of a unified nation for the first time in history. His rule brought sweeping changes: he standardized weights, measures, currency, and even the written language. He commissioned massive construction projects, including the early Great Wall, and expanded his empire's infrastructure with a vast network of roads and canals. But it was his tomb, with its underground army, that became his most ambitious project—designed to mirror his empire and ensure his dominion in the afterlife.

Imagine standing before the excavated pits for the first time, where thousands of life-sized warriors stand silently, row upon row. Their eyes seem to follow you, as if you've stepped into another world—an ancient battlefield frozen in time. Each warrior is unique, his face carefully sculpted to reflect the diversity of the emperor's army. Some appear solemn, others fierce, and each carries the weight of history on their broad shoulders.

As you walk through the excavation site, the scale of Qin Shi Huang's ambition becomes more than just a historical fact—it becomes palpable. It's a journey back through time, where the line between past and present blurs. You are no longer just a visitor to a museum; you are a witness to an emperor's eternal vision. The Terracotta Army is not merely a relic of the past—it is a testament to the power of human ambition and the eternal question of how we wish to be remembered.

This introduction merely scratches the surface of the Terracotta Army's wonders, but the journey has just begun. The deeper you dig into its story, the more you'll uncover about the man, the empire, and the incredible legacy that continues to captivate the world.

CHAPTER 1

The Life and Legacy of Qin Shi Huang

The life of Qin Shi Huang, China's First Emperor, is a story of ambition, conquest, and a relentless pursuit of power that forever changed the course of Chinese history. Born into a fragmented land of warring states, he rose to power at a young age and embarked on an unprecedented campaign to unify the country. With unmatched military prowess and strategic brilliance, he conquered six rival states, becoming the first ruler to preside over a unified China. But Qin Shi Huang's vision extended beyond the battlefield—he sought to create a centralized empire governed by laws, uniform standards, and unparalleled infrastructure. His reign was marked by sweeping reforms that shaped the political, social, and cultural landscape of China for centuries to come.

Yet, Qin Shi Huang was not content with ruling an empire. He wanted to rule forever. Obsessed with the idea of immortality, he delved into alchemy and sought the fabled elixirs of eternal life, while simultaneously building a grand tomb that would ensure his glory in the afterlife. His pursuit of immortality, combined with his harsh rule, cast a shadow over his legacy, painting him as both a visionary and a tyrant. However, despite the controversies surrounding his reign, his impact on Chinese civilization is undeniable. From the unification of China to the construction of the Great Wall, Qin Shi Huang's legacy endures as a symbol of ambition, strength, and the eternal quest for power.

The First Emperor of China

Imagine standing in a vast chamber, its walls decorated with the intricate patterns of a long-forgotten dynasty. In the center, encased in shadow, lies the figure of Qin Shi Huang, a ruler whose name would resonate through history. Born as Ying Zheng in 259 BCE, few could have predicted that this child would grow to reshape the very fabric of Chinese civilization.

At the time of his birth, China was a patchwork of warring states, each vying for power in a chaotic period known as the Warring States Era. It was a time of constant strife, where betrayal and violence were everyday occurrences. Ying Zheng, the son of King Zhuangxiang of Qin, was born into this turbulence. But from an early age, those around him could sense that he was no ordinary prince. He had an iron will, an unparalleled intelligence, and, perhaps most importantly, an unshakable belief in his destiny: to unite the warring states and rule as the first emperor of a unified China.

At the tender age of 13, Ying Zheng ascended to the throne of the Qin state, though his kingdom was still under the influence of a regent. As he matured into adulthood, Ying Zheng wasted no time consolidating power. He ruthlessly eliminated internal threats, dealing with rebellious ministers and traitorous generals who sought to weaken his reign. By the age of 22, he had claimed full control of his kingdom, and the next step of his grand vision had begun.

In the years that followed, Ying Zheng, now known as Qin Shi Huang, would embark on an unprecedented military campaign to conquer the six rival states— Han, Zhao, Wei, Chu, Yan, and Qi. It was a ruthless conquest. Entire cities were razed, and those who resisted were met with swift and brutal consequences. Yet through this destruction, Qin Shi Huang was creating something greater than the world had ever seen: a united China.

Unification of the Chinese States

Qin Shi Huang's triumph over the warring states did not happen by chance. His success was the result of calculated strategy, a powerful military, and the use of innovative weapons like the crossbow. But there was something else—an unseen force that made his victories inevitable. Qin Shi Huang was a visionary. He knew that military might alone would not cement his legacy. He needed to unify the people, not just the land.

Once his armies had subdued the last of the six states in 221 BCE, Qin Shi Huang proclaimed himself the First Emperor, a title that reflected his unprecedented achievement. No longer was China a fragmented collection of rival kingdoms. It was now one cohesive empire under the rule of a single man. And yet, for Qin Shi Huang, unification was only the beginning.

The emperor immediately set about transforming the very essence of his new empire. In a stroke of genius, he abolished the old feudal system, where noble families held control over regions. Instead, he divided the empire into administrative units that were governed by loyal officials appointed by him. This centralization of power ensured that no one could challenge his authority and that all roads led directly to the emperor.

But Qin Shi Huang's vision for unity extended beyond political reform. He recognized the importance of cultural and intellectual unity as well. Under his reign, a standardized system of writing was introduced, allowing people from different regions to communicate more easily. He also standardized measurements, currency, and even the width of cart axles, ensuring that trade and travel across the empire were smooth and consistent.

To further solidify his legacy, Qin Shi Huang commissioned ambitious infrastructure projects that were unparalleled in scale. The most famous of these was the Great Wall of China, a monumental defensive barrier intended to protect his empire from the nomadic tribes to the north. Though parts of the wall had existed before his time, Qin Shi Huang was the first to connect and extend these sections, creating what would become one of the most iconic structures in human history.

While these reforms brought unity and progress, they also brought resentment. Many scholars, particularly those who adhered to Confucian ideals, viewed Qin Shi Huang's strict legalist policies with disdain. The emperor's harsh punishments for dissent, coupled with his notorious burning of books to suppress intellectual opposition, earned him enemies among the educated class. But to Qin Shi Huang, these were necessary sacrifices. He believed that unity could only be achieved through strict control and unwavering loyalty to the state.

Qin Shi Huang's Vision of Immortality

Despite his accomplishments, there was one thing that gnawed at Qin Shi Huang's mind: death. Like many rulers before him, the emperor was haunted by the inevitability of his own mortality. But unlike others, he believed that he could conquer death just as he had conquered the warring states. His quest for immortality became an obsession, one that would lead him down strange and perilous paths.

From early in his reign, Qin Shi Huang had sought out scholars, alchemists, and magicians who claimed to hold the secret to eternal life. He commissioned expeditions to search for the mythical islands of the immortals, where it was believed that the elixir of life could be found. In one famous story, he sent an entire fleet led by an alchemist named Xu Fu to find these islands. The expedition was never heard from again.

Qin Shi Huang also turned to the burgeoning field of alchemy. He consumed potions and elixirs that were said to prolong life, many of which contained mercury—a substance we now know to be poisonous.

Ironically, his quest for immortality may have hastened his death, as the toxic substances he consumed likely weakened his body over time.

Despite his growing paranoia and obsession with avoiding death, Qin Shi Huang remained focused on his grand vision. He ordered the construction of a vast underground mausoleum, one that would ensure his glory in the afterlife. Guarded by thousands of terracotta warriors, this tomb was designed as a microcosm of his empire, with rivers of mercury flowing through its halls and a ceiling inlaid with jewels to represent the stars. The emperor may have accepted that he could not live forever in this world, but he was determined to rule in the next.

His Lasting Influence on Chinese History

Qin Shi Huang's death in 210 BCE did not mark the end of his legacy. Far from it. Though his empire would quickly fall into chaos after his passing, the structures he put in place—the centralized government, the standardized systems, the monumental infrastructure—would serve as the foundation for future dynasties.

His vision of a unified China endured, becoming the cornerstone of Chinese civilization for over two millennia. Later dynasties, such as the Han, would build upon the groundwork he laid, refining and expanding his reforms. Even today, the very name "China" (derived from "Qin") serves as a testament to his lasting influence.

But Qin Shi Huang's legacy is not without controversy. He is remembered as both a visionary and a tyrant, a ruler who achieved the impossible but at great human cost. His harsh legalist policies, which demanded absolute obedience and meted out brutal punishments for dissent, cast a long shadow over his reign. The thousands of laborers who died building his projects, the scholars who were executed for defying his edicts, and the citizens who suffered under his rigid control all stand as reminders of the dark side of his ambition.

Yet despite these contradictions, Qin Shi Huang remains a figure of fascination. His relentless pursuit of power and immortality, his sweeping reforms, and his indomitable will have made him one of the most enduring figures in world history. To this day, his terracotta army stands as a silent tribute to his grandeur—a reminder that, in the end, he achieved a form of immortality after all.

CHAPTER 2

The Construction of the Mausoleum

The construction of the mausoleum of Qin Shi Huang, the First Emperor of China, stands as one of the most remarkable feats of ancient engineering. Stretching over 56 square kilometers and hidden beneath a hill in the Shaanxi Province, this monumental tomb was intended to be more than just a final resting place—it was a microcosm of the emperor's empire, meant to last for eternity. What lay beneath the surface was far more than a simple burial chamber. It was an empire of clay warriors, chariots, horses, and weaponry, all meticulously designed to accompany the emperor in the afterlife. From its very inception, the mausoleum was imagined as the ultimate symbol of Qin Shi Huang's unrivaled power and his ambition to reign eternally, even in death.

But how did such an audacious project come to be? The mausoleum's construction began shortly after Qin Shi Huang ascended to the throne at the age of 13. The scale and vision of this project were unimaginable at the time, involving the labor of over 700,000 workers, architects, artisans, and engineers. For nearly four decades, these individuals toiled under the emperor's command, piecing together what would become an unparalleled testament to the grandiosity and mystique of ancient China. The story of how this monumental tomb came to life is not just about architecture and engineering—it is about human perseverance, imperial ambition, and a ruler's determination to defy mortality.

The Grand Project: Design and Planning

Qin Shi Huang's mausoleum was no ordinary tomb; it was an intricate reflection of his empire, meticulously planned to mirror the world above. The emperor was determined that his afterlife would mirror his reign on Earth, so the design of the mausoleum was based on the layout of the capital city of Xianyang, with inner and outer walls and elaborate palaces within. The central chamber, where the emperor's body was laid to rest, was surrounded by layers of underground passageways, each meticulously planned to symbolize different facets of his reign.

The design was driven by Qin Shi Huang's advisors and architects, but ultimately, it was his own vision that led to the scope and complexity of the project. Every detail, from the orientation of the tomb to the structure of the walls, was infused with meaning. The tomb itself was aligned along the cardinal directions, symbolizing the emperor's control over the four corners of the known world. Even the positioning of the famous Terracotta Army was deliberate—the soldiers were arranged to protect the tomb in a formation akin to the imperial guard, standing ever-vigilant at the gates of the emperor's eternal palace.

The emperor's obsession with immortality influenced every part of the planning. The inner sanctum of the tomb, where the emperor's body was buried, was said to have a ceiling decorated with pearls to resemble the stars, while the floor was a vast map of China, with rivers and seas made from flowing mercury. The belief in the power of mercury to grant eternal life further symbolized Qin Shi Huang's desire to transcend mortality. This grand vision required not only unparalleled craftsmanship but also resources and labor on a scale never before seen in human history.

The Workforce behind the Monument

Building the emperor's mausoleum was a project so immense that it required an army of laborers, artisans, and engineers, numbering over 700,000. Many of these workers were conscripted laborers, including prisoners of war, criminals, and common citizens who were drafted into service by the state. For these individuals, the construction of the mausoleum was not only a physical burden but a lifelong sentence—many never left the site, their bones now mingling with the earth beneath the monument they helped create.

Despite the grueling conditions, the scale of the workforce enabled a division of labor that ensured every aspect of the mausoleum was meticulously crafted. Artisans specialized in creating the Terracotta Warriors—each figure unique, with individual facial features, armor, and weaponry. Historians believe that the work was done in assembly-line fashion, with different groups responsible for crafting specific body parts—heads, arms, torsos—before they were assembled and painted. Similarly, teams of architects and engineers designed and constructed the underground palace, while others were responsible for digging the vast network of tunnels that connected the different chambers of the tomb.

The workforce, though large, worked under tight security and secrecy. Many of the workers were unaware of the full scope of the project, as only a select few higher-ups had knowledge of the entire mausoleum's layout and purpose. The secrecy extended beyond the emperor's death, with many of those involved in the inner sanctum's construction allegedly being buried alive to protect the tomb's secrets. It is said that the emperor, fearing that his grave would be looted, ordered the burial of these workers to prevent them from revealing the inner workings of his final resting place.

Engineering and Architectural Marvels

The sheer magnitude of the mausoleum's construction was matched only by the brilliance of its engineering. The construction of the underground palace involved advanced architectural techniques that were centuries ahead of their time. Layers of soil were compacted to form a stable structure, while the use of wooden supports helped prevent collapses. The builders also took advantage of the natural geography of the region, using the surrounding mountains and hills as natural fortifications for the tomb. The entire structure was designed to be self-contained, with tunnels and chambers that stretched for miles beneath the earth.

One of the most impressive engineering feats was the creation of the Terracotta Army itself. Each warrior, standing over six feet tall and weighing several hundred pounds, was sculpted with extraordinary precision. The figures were fired in massive kilns, some of which are believed to have been specially constructed for the project. The use of modular construction—where different body parts were made separately and later assembled—allowed for a high degree of customization while maintaining efficiency. The result was an army of lifelike soldiers, each imbued with individual characteristics that reflected the diversity of Qin Shi Huang's actual military forces.

The tomb's inner chamber, where Qin Shi Huang's body was laid to rest, was equally impressive in its design. According to historical texts, the chamber was filled with treasures and replicas of palaces, rivers, and mountains, all meant to serve the emperor in the afterlife. The most astounding feature, however, was the reported use of mercury to create flowing rivers and seas. Ancient texts describe how artisans built intricate channels to direct the flow of mercury, creating an otherworldly landscape meant to represent the emperor's dominion over the heavens and the Earth. Modern scientists have found elevated levels of mercury in the soil around the tomb, lending credence to these ancient accounts.

Secrets beneath the Tomb

Despite decades of excavation and research, much of the mausoleum remains unexcavated, shrouded in mystery. The central chamber, where Qin Shi Huang's body is believed to lie, has never been opened, due in part to concerns about preservation and the potential dangers posed by the high levels of mercury reportedly contained within. What lies beneath the tomb is the subject of much speculation, with ancient texts offering tantalizing clues.

According to the Records of the Grand Historian by Sima Qian, the central chamber was designed to be a miniature version of the emperor's empire, complete with rivers of mercury, replicas of palaces, and constellations that glimmered from the ceiling. The tomb is also rumored to contain vast treasures—gold, jade, and rare artifacts—that have remained undisturbed for over two millennia. The inner sanctum was reportedly protected by a series of traps, including crossbows rigged to fire at intruders, adding another layer of intrigue to the mystery surrounding the tomb.

As modern archaeologists continue to explore the site, new discoveries are constantly being made, but the central chamber remains elusive. For now, the secrets of Qin Shi Huang's tomb are hidden beneath layers of earth, waiting to be uncovered. The emperor's vision of immortality, both in life and in death, continues to captivate historians and adventurers alike, reminding the world of a ruler whose ambitions transcended the limits of time and space.

The story of the construction of the mausoleum is one of both grandeur and mystery—a testament to the brilliance of ancient Chinese engineering and the enduring legacy of Qin Shi Huang. His tomb, like his empire, was designed to last for eternity, and in many ways, it has. Whether the secrets beneath the tomb will ever be fully revealed remains to be seen, but one thing is certain: the Terracotta Army and the mausoleum of Qin Shi Huang stand as one of the greatest wonders of the ancient world, a timeless symbol of human ambition and the quest for immortality.

CHAPTER 3

The Discovery and Excavation

The discovery of the Terracotta Army in 1974 was not the result of a calculated search, but a twist of fate that brought the ancient world to life once more. Beneath the soil of a humble Chinese village, a few local farmers stumbled upon fragments of terracotta while digging a well. Unbeknownst to them, they had unearthed the gateway to one of the most extraordinary archaeological finds in history—a sprawling underground army of life-sized soldiers, horses, and chariots, all crafted over 2,000 years ago to guard the tomb of China's first emperor, Qin Shi Huang. What started as a simple quest for water quickly became a global sensation, captivating scholars, archaeologists, and historians alike.

The unearthing of the Terracotta Army was only the beginning. As archaeologists began the painstaking task of excavation, they encountered not only the grandeur of Qin's military vision but also a host of challenges that would take decades to overcome. From the fragility of the ancient figures to the vast scope of the mausoleum itself, the excavation was an immense undertaking that demanded both innovation and patience. This chapter delves into the thrilling story of how one of history's greatest wonders was discovered, the obstacles that arose during its excavation, and the remarkable breakthroughs that have allowed us to better understand the mysterious world of China's first emperor.

The Serendipitous Discovery in 1974

It was the spring of 1974, a year like any other in the quiet, rural expanse of Lintong District, in Shaanxi Province, China. The country was emerging from the upheaval of the Cultural Revolution, and in a small village near Mount Li, life went on as usual. Farmers, as they had done for centuries, tilled the soil, hoping for a fruitful harvest. Little did they know that beneath their feet, something far more significant than crops lay hidden—something that would change the world's understanding of ancient China forever.

One fateful morning, a group of farmers set out to dig a well to combat the region's recurring droughts. Their minds were on water, not history, as they toiled under the sun. However, what they unearthed was not the anticipated cool gush of water, but fragments of terracotta—pieces of a life-sized statue. Bewildered, they continued to dig, uncovering what seemed to be the remains of a human figure. Yet, the figure was no ordinary sculpture—it was the first of the thousands of soldiers that would later be revealed.

Word spread quickly across the village. At first, the discovery was met with confusion. The farmers had no way of knowing that they had stumbled upon one of the greatest archaeological finds of the 20th century. The local authorities were notified, and soon, a team of archaeologists arrived at the scene. What they found was beyond their wildest expectations. They had discovered an ancient army frozen in time, standing guard over the tomb of China's first emperor, Qin Shi Huang.

The initial shock was palpable. Here, in the earth beneath their fields, lay a silent army—rows upon rows of life-sized terracotta soldiers, each with unique facial expressions, standing as if ready for battle. The discovery was entirely serendipitous, and yet it felt as though history had chosen that moment to reveal itself to the world.

Early Excavation Challenges

Once the significance of the discovery became apparent, the Chinese government acted quickly to protect the site. But the process was anything but smooth. Archaeology in the 1970s, particularly in China, was not equipped to handle an excavation of such unprecedented scale and complexity. The initial challenge was simply comprehending the enormity of what lay buried. The few statues uncovered by the farmers were just a small glimpse into a vast underground world.

The early excavation teams faced a myriad of difficulties. For one, the sheer size of the site was overwhelming. As more and more soldiers were unearthed, it became clear that this was not a single chamber but a sprawling necropolis, extending far beyond the initial discovery. Estimates quickly grew, predicting that the site could house as many as 8,000 soldiers, along with horses, chariots, and weapons.

Another challenge was the fragility of the terracotta figures. Although they had remained buried for over two millennia, exposure to air and light posed a significant threat to their preservation. Many of the figures were found broken or incomplete, damaged by the pressures of time and earth. The task of excavating these statues without causing further harm required delicate, precise work. Teams of archaeologists had to carefully remove layers of soil while ensuring that each fragment was meticulously cataloged and preserved.

Adding to the complexity was the lack of advanced preservation techniques. The figures were originally painted in vibrant colors, but once exposed to the air, the paint began to flake off almost immediately. This presented an enormous dilemma: how could the archaeologists excavate the site without destroying its most striking features? For many of the early years, this remained an unsolved problem, leading to the painful reality that much of the original artistry was lost.

Political factors also complicated the excavation efforts. China in the 1970s was still grappling with the aftereffects of the Cultural Revolution, and resources were scarce. Archaeology, while important, competed with other national priorities, making it difficult to secure the funding and materials necessary for proper excavation. Nevertheless, the Chinese government understood the importance of the find, and efforts to uncover the Terracotta Army proceeded, though slowly and with great caution.

Unveiling the Full Extent of the Site

As the excavation moved forward, it became increasingly clear that the discovery was far more than a burial chamber; it was a vast subterranean complex, constructed to immortalize Emperor Qin Shi Huang's reign in ways that defied imagination. The site was divided into multiple pits, each revealing a new chapter in the story of this ancient army.

Pit 1, the largest of the excavated areas, was where the first warriors had been discovered. It stretched across more than 14,000 square meters—an expanse that could house entire city blocks. Within its depths stood row upon row of infantry soldiers, arranged in precise formations as though awaiting the command to march into battle. The magnitude of the site was staggering. Archaeologists marveled at the level of organization and planning that had gone into its construction. This was not a random collection of statues; it was a carefully orchestrated monument to the power and military might of Qin Shi Huang.

Pit 2 was no less impressive, housing a mixture of cavalry, infantry, archers, and war chariots. The figures here were even more intricate, each warrior crafted with individual characteristics, down to the folds of their robes and the expressions on their faces. Pit 2 offered insight into the different roles within Qin's army, showcasing the diversity of his forces.

Pit 3, the smallest of the excavated areas, was believed to serve as the command center for the army. Within it stood officers and generals, their more elaborate uniforms and armor denoting their higher rank. This pit provided a rare glimpse into the hierarchy and organization of Qin's military apparatus.

As more pits were uncovered, the scale of the project grew ever larger. It became clear that the mausoleum complex was not just a burial site but an entire underground kingdom, constructed to serve the emperor in the afterlife. The figures weren't limited to soldiers; artisans, acrobats, musicians, and officials were also discovered, adding to the richness of the site's cultural significance. Each discovery deepened our understanding of the emperor's vision of his eternal reign.

Archaeological Breakthroughs

Over the years, as technology advanced, so too did the methods used to excavate and study the Terracotta Army. One of the most significant breakthroughs came in the form of 3D scanning and imaging technology, which allowed archaeologists to map the site without disturbing its fragile contents. This non-invasive approach provided a clearer picture of the extent of the mausoleum and helped researchers develop more effective preservation techniques.

Another key advancement was in the field of conservation. The early loss of the figures' painted surfaces had been a major blow, but by the late 20th century, scientists had developed methods to preserve the remaining pigments. Using specialized chemicals and advanced climate control techniques, they were able to halt the degradation of the paint, preserving the statues in a more authentic state. While much of the original color had been lost, these advancements marked a turning point in the ongoing effort to protect and restore the Terracotta Army.

The excavation of the site also led to a greater understanding of Qin Shi Huang's tomb itself, which remains largely unexcavated. According to historical records, the emperor's actual burial chamber lies beneath a massive mound near the site of the Terracotta Army. Legend has it that the tomb contains rivers of mercury and other treasures, but fears of damaging the site—and the toxic risks posed by the mercury—have kept archaeologists from probing too deeply. Even today, much of the emperor's mausoleum remains shrouded in mystery, waiting for the day when technology will allow for a safe and thorough exploration.

The discovery of the Terracotta Army has also sparked ongoing debates about its purpose. Was it purely a funerary art, designed to protect the emperor in the afterlife, or did it serve a more political or spiritual function? Some scholars believe the army was intended to convey a message of power, not just to the spirits of the underworld, but to future generations. Others suggest that the army reflects the emperor's deep-seated fear of death and his obsession with immortality.

Whatever the true purpose, the excavation of the Terracotta Army has provided an unparalleled window into the mind of one of history's most ambitious rulers. Through careful excavation, analysis, and preservation, archaeologists continue to unravel the secrets of this ancient wonder, bringing us closer to understanding the complex legacy of Qin Shi Huang.

As visitors from around the world walk among the silent soldiers today, they are reminded of the serendipity of that fateful day in 1974 and the extraordinary journey that followed. From a simple farmer's well to one of the greatest archaeological discoveries of all time, the story of the Terracotta Army is one of awe, perseverance, and the enduring mysteries of history.

CHAPTER 4

The Significance of the Terracotta Army

The Terracotta Army is not merely a collection of ancient statues; it is a profound symbol of an era, a culture, and a ruler whose ambition reshaped China. Buried in secrecy for over two millennia, this army of over 8,000 life-sized soldiers, horses, and chariots was created to guard the tomb of Emperor Qin Shi Huang and ensure his dominance extended into the afterlife. Its sheer scale and intricate detail offer a glimpse into the might of the Qin Dynasty, reflecting not only the emperor's military power but also his far-reaching vision of immortality. As a testament to the artistry, strategy, and political ideals of ancient China, the Terracotta Army stands as one of the most significant archaeological discoveries of the 20th century. Its discovery has changed our understanding of Chinese history and offers an unparalleled window into the ancient world.

Beyond its historical and artistic value, the significance of the Terracotta Army extends to broader cultural and philosophical dimensions. Each soldier, uniquely crafted, is not just a representation of military might but a reflection of the societal structure and the emperor's role as the unifier of China. The army's creation, a massive project requiring vast resources and labor, speaks to the emperor's centralization of power and the sacrifices made to fulfill his vision. Moreover, the Terracotta Army reveals the ancient Chinese belief in the afterlife, where the material world is replicated to ensure a smooth transition to the next. Through this army, we see the convergence of politics, religion, and art, making the Terracotta Army not just a historical relic but a timeless symbol of humanity's quest for power, legacy, and immortality.

Symbolism in the Afterlife

The year is 210 BCE. Imagine standing in the heart of a vast burial complex, the air thick with the weight of destiny and immortality. In the middle of this monumental site lies the mausoleum of Qin Shi Huang, the first Emperor of China, a man who sought to conquer not only the living world but the realms of the dead. The Terracotta Army, which surrounds his tomb in vast numbers, stands as silent guardians to his soul, protectors of a king's eternal journey.

To fully grasp the significance of this army, we must step back into the mind of Qin Shi Huang. His quest for immortality was not a casual obsession—it consumed him. Legend tells of his relentless search for the elixir of life, his fear of death looming like a shadow. When it became clear that he could not live forever in the physical realm, he turned his focus toward the afterlife. In ancient Chinese beliefs, the afterlife was not a place of rest but an extension of life. If a man was a ruler in this world, he would continue to rule in the next. But to rule, he needed an army.

The Terracotta Army is more than a collection of statues; it is a grand statement of the emperor's desire to maintain his empire beyond death. These thousands of life-sized warriors, horses, and chariots were built not just as symbols, but as functional elements of his afterlife court. Each soldier was crafted with unique features, from expressions to armor, echoing the emperor's belief that his armies would continue to serve him, not just as abstract representations but as living, breathing soldiers in the world beyond.

The symbolism runs deep. These soldiers were not carved from the finest jade or gold, but from clay—a material connected to the earth, representing both creation and mortality. The clay warriors symbolize the bond between the emperor's mortal life and his divine aspirations. The scale of the army, meticulously arranged in battle formations, shows how Qin Shi Huang viewed death: not as an ending but as a continuation of the order, control, and power that defined his rule.

In ancient China, rulers often surrounded themselves with servants, concubines, and retainers in death, sacrificing living humans to accompany them to the afterlife. However, Qin Shi Huang broke from this tradition. Instead of sacrificing thousands of living soldiers, he chose to have them represented in clay—an action that spoke of both pragmatism and foresight. He ensured that his dominion would not end with his final breath, that his reign would persist, unchallenged, in the mysterious world that awaited him.

Representing Qin Shi Huang's Military Power

To understand the sheer might of Qin Shi Huang's military power, one only needs to look into the faces of his clay warriors. Imagine row after row of meticulously crafted soldiers, each standing over six feet tall, their armor chiseled with precision, weapons in hand, eyes fixed on an unseen enemy. The sight would have been both awe-inspiring and intimidating—exactly as the emperor intended.

The soldiers of the Terracotta Army are a testament to Qin Shi Huang's unparalleled military dominance. Under his leadership, China was unified for the first time in history, following centuries of warring states. His army was the most feared and revered force of its time, with cutting-edge weaponry, strategic formations, and military tactics that had never been seen before. The Terracotta Army immortalizes this force, preserving in clay the essence of what made his reign so powerful.

Each soldier's individuality—no two faces are the same—represents the diversity within his real army. From hardened veterans to young recruits, archers, foot soldiers, cavalry, and officers, every rank is represented, just as they were in life. This was no haphazard collection of statues; it was a painstakingly detailed recreation of his military machine, which conquered all who stood before it.

Even the weapons they held were not mere replicas; many were actual bronze swords, spears, and crossbows, designed to function if ever needed. These were not ornamental; they were a reminder that Qin Shi Huang's power was not just symbolic. His warriors were armed and ready to fight even in death, reinforcing the emperor's belief in his own invincibility. Through the Terracotta Army, Qin Shi Huang proclaimed to the world that his military might was eternal, that no foe—earthly or otherwise—could stand against him.

This grand display was not just for the benefit of the emperor's soul but also a message to those still living. The Terracotta Army conveyed a powerful image to future generations of Chinese rulers: here lies a man who united the warring states through sheer force of will, a leader whose military prowess could not be extinguished, even by death.

Cultural and Political Implications

The Terracotta Army is more than a display of military might or an emperor's obsession with the afterlife. It stands as a pivotal cultural and political symbol in Chinese history, reflecting the ambition, vision, and complexity of Qin Shi Huang's reign.

Politically, the construction of the army was part of a broader strategy to legitimize Qin Shi Huang's rule. His reign marked the transition from the chaotic Warring States period to a unified China under one emperor. To ensure his power was unquestioned, Qin Shi Huang needed to project an image of invincibility, both in life and death. The Terracotta Army was part of that image—an unspoken declaration that his dynasty was ordained by the heavens, destined to rule all of China and, by extension, the afterlife.

Culturally, the Terracotta Army represents a shift in the concept of rulership in China. Qin Shi Huang was not content with being remembered as a mere king or warlord. He sought to transcend the boundaries of time, to ensure his legacy would endure for millennia. The creation of such an extraordinary and grand burial complex spoke to a fundamental change in how Chinese rulers viewed their place in history. No longer were they simply mortal beings tasked with ruling for a finite period; they were seen as divine, eternal figures whose influence would last for all eternity.

The significance of this army also reflects the cultural values of Confucianism and legalism that were prevalent during the emperor's reign. While Confucian scholars criticized the emperor for his harsh rule and massive building projects, the legalist doctrine that underpinned his government emphasized order, discipline, and control—all traits embodied by the meticulously organized army of clay warriors.

Furthermore, the army has become an enduring symbol of national pride in modern China. It stands as a reminder of China's rich cultural heritage and its contributions to world civilization. The discovery of the Terracotta Army brought international attention to

China's ancient history, prompting scholars and archaeologists to reevaluate its role in shaping global history. The army became not just a national treasure but a symbol of China's longstanding influence, a cultural and political asset that reinforces the country's historical significance.

A Global Historical Treasure

Since its discovery in 1974 by a group of farmers digging a well, the Terracotta Army has captured the imagination of people across the globe. What started as a local archaeological find quickly became one of the most important discoveries of the 20th century. The site has since been named a UNESCO World Heritage site, with millions of visitors flocking to Xi'an each year to witness this awe-inspiring wonder.

The global significance of the Terracotta Army cannot be overstated. It offers a rare glimpse into the life and beliefs of an ancient civilization, showcasing the artistry, craftsmanship, and technological advancements of the Qin Dynasty. For historians, the army provides valuable insights into the military organization, weaponry, and burial practices of ancient China. For archaeologists, it offers an ongoing mystery, as new discoveries continue to emerge from the site.

But beyond the academic interest, the Terracotta Army has touched people on a deeper, more emotional level. The lifelike expressions on the faces of the soldiers remind us that history is not just a series of distant events but a collection of human experiences. These statues, frozen in time, carry the weight of an ancient emperor's dreams and ambitions, yet they also reflect universal themes of power, mortality, and the desire for legacy. Standing before them, one cannot help but wonder about the lives of the craftsmen who sculpted these warriors, the soldiers who inspired them, and the emperor who believed so deeply in his own immortality.

As a global treasure, the Terracotta Army has transcended its origins, becoming a symbol of humanity's quest to understand its past and shape its future. The meticulous detail in each warrior, the scale of the project, and the sheer vision behind it have made the Terracotta Army a touchstone for discussions on art, history, and the human spirit. Exhibitions of the warriors have traveled the world, allowing people from all corners of the globe to connect with this ancient story, marveling at the ingenuity and ambition of one of history's greatest civilizations.

The Terracotta Army is more than just an archaeological site or a historical artifact—it is a bridge between the ancient and the modern, a testament to the enduring legacy of a single emperor's vision. As long as the warriors stand, they will continue to tell the story of Qin Shi Huang's reign, reminding us of the power of human imagination and the lengths to which we will go to leave our mark on the world.

CHAPTER 5

The Soldiers: Their Roles and Functions

As you step into the heart of the Terracotta Army, it becomes clear that these soldiers are not just statues, but representations of a complex and highly organized military force. Each warrior, standing silently in formation, is a testament to the might and discipline of Qin Shi Huang's empire. From the archers poised with precision to the generals exuding authority, every soldier embodies a specific role within this massive army, reflecting the intricate military hierarchy of the time. Their lifelike expressions, varied postures, and meticulously crafted armor suggest that these are not mere replicas, but rather a direct extension of the emperor's formidable army—a force designed to protect him not only in life, but for eternity.

Yet, the roles and functions of these soldiers go beyond their impressive appearance. Each type of warrior within the army—whether foot soldiers, archers, or cavalrymen—was deliberately positioned to serve a strategic purpose. These figures were carefully arranged to mirror the military tactics that helped Qin

Shi Huang unify China. The craftsmanship behind each soldier reflects a deep understanding of combat, discipline, and the importance of order. In this chapter, we will explore the distinct roles of these soldiers, delving into the significance of their positions, their armor, and their weapons, and uncovering how each one was integral to the emperor's grand vision of eternal protection.

The Different Types of Warriors

Imagine walking into a vast chamber where thousands of silent sentinels stand in perfect rows, frozen in time yet radiating a palpable sense of duty and vigilance. These figures, the soldiers of the Terracotta Army, are not mere statues. Each one, meticulously crafted with unique facial expressions, body language, and attire, represents an ancient warrior prepared to protect their emperor, Qin Shi Huang, in the afterlife. They were created to serve him eternally, and in doing so, they mirror the structured ranks of an ancient army—a reflection of the grand military force that once helped unify China under one ruler.

But who were these warriors? What roles did they serve, and why was it so important that they be so varied in appearance and rank?

The Terracotta Army is composed of several distinct types of soldiers, each playing a unique role in this vast clay battalion. First, we meet the infantrymen—the backbone of any army. These foot soldiers, positioned in the front lines, are depicted standing firm and ready for battle. They come in various forms: some hold spears, others wield crossbows, and a few are unarmed, perhaps once grasping wooden or bronze weapons that have since rotted away. The infantry represents the core strength of the emperor's forces, a crucial element in both offensive and defensive military strategies. Each infantryman wears an expression of determination, hinting at their readiness to face the unknown.

Behind the infantry, you'll find the archers. These soldiers are depicted either kneeling or standing, poised to unleash a volley of arrows. Their placement in the ranks reflects their real-life role: to strike from a distance, softening enemy lines before the infantry engaged in close combat. The kneeling archers, with their sturdy postures, suggest a readiness to fire at a moment's notice, while the standing archers offer a sense of vigilance, their sharp eyes scanning the horizon for danger. The fact that the artists captured the archers mid-action speaks volumes about the military precision of the time. Every archer was a specialist, trained to strike with lethal accuracy.

Among the most awe-inspiring figures are the cavalrymen. These warriors sit astride life-sized terracotta horses, as if ready to charge into battle at the emperor's command. Their horses, with finely detailed bridles and manes, embody the elegance and power of these vital military units. The cavalry was the emperor's fast-moving strike force, capable of flanking the enemy or chasing down retreating foes. The terracotta cavalrymen wear helmets and armor, their hands gripping the reins, their faces marked with resolve. Each cavalryman appears to share a special connection with his horse, almost as though man and beast are a single unit of battle strength.

Then come the officers and generals, distinguishable by their more ornate armor, elaborate headgear, and commanding presence. These figures, placed strategically throughout the army, demonstrate the importance of leadership within the ranks. Their solemn faces suggest wisdom and experience, qualities essential to guiding a large army. Some wear expressions of quiet contemplation, others seem to exude an air of supreme confidence. The generals, standing tall above the rank-and-file soldiers, were responsible for devising battle strategies and leading the emperor's army to victory. Their role was not just one of brute strength but also of keen intellect and strategic thinking.

Together, these soldiers form a complex and layered military force, each figure carefully designed to represent a specific function within the emperor's grand vision of afterlife protection. Every warrior, from the lowest infantryman to the highest-ranking general, had a purpose, and their combined strength was intended to ensure Qin Shi Huang's reign extended beyond death.

Weapons and Armor

The soldiers were not just posed in battle formations—they were armed to the teeth. The terracotta warriors, as detailed as they are, would not have been complete without their weapons, and here the craftsmanship shines just as brightly as in the figures themselves.

The weapons found in the tomb were not just ceremonial. They were real, battle-ready instruments made of bronze, and many remained surprisingly well-preserved, a testament to the advanced metalworking techniques of ancient China. Bronze swords, spears, and crossbows—tools designed to pierce armor and skin—were all part of the arsenal. The sharpness of these weapons, even after over two millennia, demonstrates the Chinese mastery of weapon crafting, and their attention to detail in preparing for battle, whether in life or the afterlife.

Each soldier, depending on his rank and role, was equipped with specific gear. Infantrymen bore spears and short swords, ideal for close combat. Some of the soldiers also carried long pikes, suggesting their readiness to defend against mounted attacks. The archers, meanwhile, were armed with crossbows, which were a technological marvel of their time, capable of shooting arrows with deadly precision over long distances. The crossbow mechanism, designed to release bolts with significant force, was a key factor in the military dominance of Qin Shi Huang's forces.

The cavalrymen, riding their lifelike terracotta horses, were often armed with long swords or lances, designed for slashing and charging into enemy ranks. Their role as fast-moving attackers required weapons that were both durable and versatile, able to withstand the speed and intensity of cavalry combat.

Armor was equally important, protecting these soldiers from the strikes of enemy forces. The terracotta figures were depicted wearing either light or heavy armor, depending on their role. Infantrymen wore protective plates covering their torsos, while generals and officers donned more elaborate and extensive armor, symbolizing their higher status and the need for extra protection in command positions. The armor was crafted with a careful balance between mobility and defense, allowing the soldiers to move quickly in battle while still being shielded from enemy attacks.

The attention to detail in the armor was meticulous, right down to the intricate patterns and designs that adorned the plates. These designs were not merely decorative—they symbolized rank, status, and function. In an army where every warrior had a specific role, even their armor conveyed their place in the hierarchy.

Artistry and Craftsmanship

The Terracotta Army is not just a historical artifact; it is a masterpiece of ancient artistry and craftsmanship. Each soldier, horse, and weapon is the result of a painstaking creative process, one that involved thousands of artisans and craftsmen working under the emperor's command.

The level of individual detail in each figure is extraordinary. No two soldiers look exactly alike—a feat considering the vast number of warriors unearthed. The facial features of each soldier are unique, suggesting that the craftsmen might have been inspired by real soldiers who served in Qin Shi Huang's army. Some figures have high cheekbones and narrow eyes, others rounder faces and fuller lips. The individuality of each face suggests an artistic effort to portray not just an army, but the humanity within it.

Even the smallest details—like the folds in a soldier's robes or the knots in his armor—were crafted with immense precision. The hands of the archers are carefully sculpted to show the tension of drawing a bowstring. The horses' muscles ripple under their clay skin, capturing the raw power of these animals as they prepare for battle. These are not static figures; they are dynamic, caught in the midst of action, their forms imbued with life and movement.

The process of creating these figures involved an innovative assembly-line technique, where different artisans specialized in different parts of the figure. Heads, torsos, limbs, and hands were created separately and then assembled, allowing for a degree of mass production while still maintaining individual uniqueness. This method enabled the rapid creation of thousands of figures while preserving the high level of artistry that makes the Terracotta Army so remarkable.

But the artistry didn't stop at the sculpting. The figures were originally painted in vibrant colors, though much of the paint has faded over time. Traces of pigments found on the statues reveal that the soldiers once wore brightly colored robes, with details like facial hair and eyes painstakingly painted to bring the figures even closer to life. This use of color would have made the army even more striking, creating a vivid, lifelike scene of warriors poised for battle.

The Role of Each Soldier in the Army

The soldiers of the Terracotta Army were more than just a representation of Qin Shi Huang's military might—they were part of a larger narrative about loyalty, duty, and eternal service. In life, the emperor's army had fought to unite China, creating the foundation for one of the most powerful empires in history. In death, these soldiers were charged with protecting him, ensuring that his rule extended into the afterlife.

Each soldier had a specific role to play, both in the structure of the army and in the afterlife narrative. The infantrymen, positioned at the front of the formations, represented the emperor's first line of defense, ready to meet any threat head-on. Behind them, the archers provided cover, their crossbows primed to pick off enemies from a distance. The cavalry, swift and decisive, was prepared to outmaneuver the emperor's foes, while the generals and officers guided the troops with wisdom and strategy.

In a broader sense, the Terracotta Army was a symbol of the emperor's vision of immortality. Qin Shi Huang believed that by replicating his army in clay, he could recreate the power he held in life and carry it with him into the afterlife. Each soldier, in their precise role, was a testament to this vision—a vision of unyielding power, eternal loyalty, and a seamless transition from life to death.

This grand project, spanning decades and involving untold numbers of artisans and laborers, was not just about the physical protection of an emperor's tomb. It was about ensuring that the emperor's legacy would endure for all eternity. Every terracotta soldier, horse, and chariot stood as a reminder that the emperor's reign, though it had ended in the mortal world, would persist forever in the afterlife. Each soldier played a part in this grand orchestration of power, and their individual roles were essential to maintaining the integrity of the emperor's vision.

The **infantry,** as the bulk of the army, symbolized strength in numbers, just as they had in life when they overwhelmed enemies with sheer force. Their positioning in the front lines was strategic—they were the first to engage the enemy, just as they would have been in life, and they were meant to form an impenetrable shield around their emperor in the afterlife. Their steadfast posture and alert expressions speak to their readiness, even in the stillness of the tomb, to protect their leader at any cost.

The **archers**, with their specialized weapons, represented precision and skill. In battle, they were the soldiers who could strike from a distance, targeting enemies before they could get too close. This element of the army was crucial not just for offense, but for defense as well, creating a buffer zone that protected the rest of the troops. In the afterlife, their role was no less vital—they stood poised to defend the emperor from unseen dangers, their keen eyes ever watchful.

The **cavalry,** depicted mid-gallop or holding the reins of their horses, embodied speed and agility. In life, cavalry units were the elite forces, often used to flank the enemy or chase down fleeing opponents. Their ability to move quickly across the battlefield made them a critical component of any successful military campaign. In the afterlife, they maintained this role, standing ready to ride into battle at a moment's notice, their horses as alert and powerful as the warriors who rode them.

Finally, the **officers and generals** held the key roles of leadership and strategy. They were not just warriors; they were thinkers, planners, and commanders who had earned their rank through years of experience and proven success in battle. Their presence in the Terracotta Army signifies the importance of order and discipline, even in the afterlife. Without leadership, an army is nothing more than a disorganized mob. These generals ensured that the emperor's forces remained cohesive, unified, and capable of defending him from any threat, no matter how long the journey through the afterlife might be.

Each rank, each soldier, was not just a piece of clay— they were a piece of the emperor's soul, a fragment of his power that he believed would protect him for eternity. And though they were created for a specific purpose, their roles have transcended their original function. Today, they stand as symbols of an empire's ambition, its military might, and the emperor's belief in immortality. They remind us that, in ancient China, power was not just about ruling the land—it was about ruling the afterlife.

These soldiers, though long since silenced, continue to speak to us through the ages. Their carefully crafted forms tell stories of a time when emperors sought to control not just life, but death itself. Their weapons, though rusted, still reflect the brilliance of ancient Chinese metallurgy. Their faces, each unique, remind us of the individuals who made up this incredible force—real people, real warriors, now immortalized in clay.

As we look upon the Terracotta Army today, we see more than just statues. We see an ancient world brought to life through the artistry and craftsmanship of countless artisans. We see an emperor's dream of eternal power, manifest in the form of an army that stands ready to serve him forever. And in each figure, from the infantryman to the general, we see the enduring legacy of a time when the boundary between life and death was not just a transition, but a continuation of a ruler's reign.

In this way, the Terracotta soldiers, in their roles and functions, not only protected their emperor—they ensured that his name, his vision, and his empire would be remembered for millennia to come.

CHAPTER 6

The Chariots and Horses of the Terracotta Army

The sight of rows upon rows of terracotta soldiers is enough to leave any visitor in awe, but standing among these warriors are perhaps the most majestic figures of all: the horses and chariots. These life-sized animals, poised with a sense of readiness and strength, amplify the grandeur of the army they accompany. Crafted with an astonishing level of detail, from the musculature of the horses to the intricacies of the chariots' framework, these figures reflect the meticulous artistry of the artisans of Qin Shi Huang's reign. The horses appear alert, their eyes wide and their ears pricked, as if awaiting the command to charge into battle. The chariots, some still in remarkable condition, represent the height of ancient Chinese engineering, showcasing both military might and the emperor's mastery over his vast empire. These creations symbolize not only the physical power that Qin Shi Huang wielded during his lifetime but also his strategic vision—one that extended beyond the earthly realm and into the afterlife.

More than just objects, these horses and chariots are the embodiment of Qin Shi Huang's enduring ambition and vision of eternal rule. In his quest for immortality, the emperor envisioned his afterlife as a continuation of his imperial dominion on Earth, and the presence of these chariots and horses emphasizes the scale of his authority. They were not mere symbols of transportation or warfare; they were an extension of his reign, meant to ensure his supremacy even in death. The precision and care taken to recreate such lifelike figures also speak to the emperor's insistence on perfection and control—traits that defined his rule. These majestic figures, standing silently among the terracotta soldiers, serve as a powerful reminder of the emperor's desire for immortality, his understanding of military power, and the lengths he was willing to go to secure his legacy, not just in this world, but in the world beyond.

The Art of Crafting the Horse

The craftsmanship behind the terracotta horses is nothing short of extraordinary. Standing life-sized, these equine figures were modeled after real horses that once galloped through the vast plains of China, carrying soldiers into battle and pulling chariots through imperial processions. Sculptors of the time were tasked with capturing every detail, from the rippling muscles beneath their hides to the flare of their nostrils. Each horse was a testament to the artisans' deep understanding of anatomy and movement.

These horses were not identical copies; much like the soldiers, each was crafted with slight variations in posture, facial expression, and detail. Some horses stand tall and proud, their heads held high, while others appear as if they're mid-trot, their hooves raised. The variation brings them to life, making it easy to imagine them in motion, galloping across a battlefield or trotting into the afterlife with their imperial master.

One of the most remarkable aspects of these creations is how they combine artistry with utility. These were not just ceremonial figures but representations of real war horses—animals that played an integral role in Qin Shi Huang's conquests. The emperor's artisans were well aware of the symbolism attached to horses in Chinese culture. They were seen as creatures of strength, speed, and endurance, and by placing them alongside his army, the emperor ensured that his power would be well-protected in both this life and the next.

Imagine, for a moment, the process of crafting these horses. In an age without the machinery and technology we take for granted today, skilled artisans shaped each figure by hand. Layer upon layer of clay was molded and smoothed, while intricate details, such as the horse's mane and tail, were etched with tools.

The process would have been time-consuming, and the pressure to achieve perfection immense. These were no ordinary works of art; they were creations meant to serve the first emperor of China in the afterlife—a man whose ambition was as vast as his empire. For Qin Shi Huang, nothing less than the best would suffice.

The Functionality of Chariots in Battle

If the horses were symbols of strength and endurance, the chariots were the vehicles that carried the emperor's power across the battlefield. To understand the significance of these chariots in Qin Shi Huang's mausoleum, we must first understand their importance in ancient Chinese warfare.

During the Warring States period, when Qin Shi Huang rose to power, chariots were a key component of military strategy. They provided a platform for archers and spearmen, allowing them to engage enemies from a higher vantage point while maintaining speed and mobility. The combination of horse-drawn speed and the height advantage made chariots a devastating weapon on the battlefield.

The terracotta chariots found in the emperor's tomb reflect this vital role. Modeled in incredible detail, they were built with precision, showcasing the complex engineering of the time. Each chariot was constructed with a wooden frame, reinforced with metal fittings and wheels designed for maneuverability. The horses pulling these chariots were poised as if ready to charge, their bodies full of energy, their eyes wide with purpose.

In battle, these chariots could turn the tide of a confrontation. An archer stationed on a chariot could rain arrows down on enemy troops from a distance, while spearmen could fend off close-range attackers. The chariot itself, sturdy and fast, allowed the soldiers to cover vast distances quickly, repositioning as the battle demanded. It was a tool of war, yes, but it was also a representation of tactical brilliance.

Qin Shi Huang's military campaigns relied heavily on the use of chariots, and it's no surprise that they would feature prominently in his mausoleum. These chariots were not just symbols of his earthly victories but also his hope for continued dominance in the afterlife. In the grand scheme of the emperor's vision, these chariots, along with the soldiers and horses, were a vital part of his eternal army.

Imagine the sound of those chariots thundering across the plains, the clatter of wheels and hooves merging with the battle cries of soldiers. It's easy to see why Qin Shi Huang, a ruler obsessed with both military might and immortality, would want these powerful tools at his side for eternity.

Horses and chariots were not just functional in ancient China—they were symbols of status, power, and wealth. The presence of these figures in Qin Shi Huang's tomb speaks to more than just military prowess; it speaks to the emperor's desire to project his dominance across all aspects of life, even in death

In Chinese culture, horses have long been revered as noble creatures, representing loyalty, freedom, and speed. They were prized possessions, often given as gifts to emperors and high-ranking officials. The more horses one owned, the greater their status. By including life-sized horses in his mausoleum, Qin Shi Huang was asserting his place not only as a military leader but as a ruler of unparalleled status.

Chariots, too, carried significant symbolic weight. In the emperor's time, they were not merely used for war but also for ceremonial purposes. Chariots were often part of grand processions, displaying the emperor's wealth and power to his people. The terracotta chariots in the mausoleum, therefore, were not just tools for battle in the afterlife but representations of the emperor's grandeur and majesty. They were a way for him to remind the world—even in death—of his supreme authority.

The symbolism extends even further. The positioning of the horses and chariots in the mausoleum suggests a deeper meaning. These figures were placed strategically, with the chariots leading the charge and the horses poised for action, ready to carry the emperor into the afterlife. It was as if Qin Shi Huang was preparing for one final, eternal battle—a battle not for territory or power on Earth, but for supremacy in the afterlife.

In a sense, the horses and chariots represent the emperor's unyielding ambition. They are a reminder that Qin Shi Huang was not content with ruling a unified China; he sought to control the very forces of life and death. The grandeur of these figures serves as a testament to his belief in his own immortality, his desire to be remembered as the greatest ruler in history.

The Role of Cavalry in the Emperor's Vision

Qin Shi Huang's vision of an eternal empire was one built on the foundations of military strength. In life, he relied on his army to conquer and unify China, and in death, he intended to bring that army with him. The inclusion of cavalry in his terracotta army was no accident—it was a deliberate reflection of the critical role that mounted troops played in his military strategy.

Cavalry, which included both horse-mounted soldiers and charioteers, was essential in Qin Shi Huang's campaigns. Mounted troops provided the speed and mobility needed to outmaneuver enemies, while chariots offered a mobile platform for launching attacks. The combination of these two forces gave the emperor a tactical advantage that helped him secure victory after victory.

In the mausoleum, the cavalry stands as a symbol of Qin Shi Huang's military genius. The horses, poised and ready, are more than just transport for the soldiers—they are integral components of the emperor's fighting force. These mounted troops were the elite of the elite, the warriors who could strike fear into the hearts of enemies with their speed, precision, and power.

The role of cavalry in the emperor's vision for the afterlife is clear: they were his vanguard, the force that would protect him in the next world as they had in this one. By including cavalry in his terracotta army, Qin Shi Huang was ensuring that he would have the mobility and strength needed to maintain his rule beyond the grave.

But beyond their practical role, the horses and chariots in the mausoleum also reflect the emperor's broader vision of his empire. Qin Shi Huang saw himself as the eternal ruler, a man destined to conquer not only the mortal world but also the spiritual realm. His terracotta army, with its horses and chariots leading the charge, was a manifestation of that vision—a vision of an empire that would last forever.

CHAPTER 7

The Preservation and Restoration Efforts

The Terracotta Army, a masterpiece of human ingenuity, is not just a relic of the past; it is a living testament to history's enduring power. Over two millennia since its creation, these silent warriors still captivate the world with their stoic expressions, intricate craftsmanship, and sheer magnitude. Yet, their continued presence is nothing short of a miracle. When the Terracotta Army was first unearthed in 1974, many of the statues had already suffered significant damage due to exposure, looting, and natural decay over time. Their pigments, which once brought them to life in vibrant reds, greens, and purples, faded away quickly upon contact with the air. The delicate nature of these figures posed immense challenges to the archaeologists and conservators tasked with their preservation. However, the story of the Terracotta Army's survival is also the story of human persistence and ingenuity—just as monumental as their original creation.

Over the past several decades, preservation efforts have evolved into a global collaboration involving cutting-edge technology and shared expertise. Specialists from China and around the world have worked together to develop innovative techniques, such as 3D scanning and restoration methods that respect the warriors' original craftsmanship while protecting their integrity. Additionally, international teams have focused on preventing further damage by controlling the environmental conditions within the excavation sites, such as humidity and temperature. Perhaps most impressive is the ongoing research into recreating the vivid colors that once adorned these soldiers, as scientists seek to restore not just the form, but the life that once animated these figures. The determination to preserve this monumental achievement speaks to the universal respect for cultural heritage and the shared responsibility of ensuring the lessons of history are not forgotten.

Challenges of Time and Exposure

The moment the Terracotta Army was unearthed, it faced a new kind of battle—one against the very forces of nature that had preserved it for over two millennia. The warriors, originally hidden beneath layers of earth, were never meant to see the light of day in the way they have. Exposed to air, moisture, and even human touch, the soldiers began to deteriorate almost immediately after their excavation.

One of the greatest challenges is the fragility of the paint that adorned many of the soldiers. When discovered, some of the warriors still bore traces of bright pigments—shades of red, blue, green, and purple—that brought them to life. However, within minutes of exposure to air, these colors began to fade and peel. The lacquer used to attach the paint to the terracotta would shrink and curl, causing the precious hues to disintegrate before the archaeologists' eyes. It was as if the soldiers were retreating back into the shadows of time, their vibrant details vanishing just as quickly as they were revealed.

Another pressing challenge was the structural damage the soldiers had endured over centuries. Many of the warriors were found in pieces—arms detached, heads separated from bodies, and torsos broken. The underground vaults, which had housed the army, were not immune to natural disasters like floods, earthquakes, and soil pressure. Over time, these forces had caused cracks, collapses, and shifts in the ground, leaving a puzzle of terracotta fragments for archaeologists and restorers to piece back together.

But perhaps the most insidious threat came from microorganisms. Bacteria and fungi, which thrive in the damp and dark conditions of underground chambers, began to feast on the terracotta, slowly eroding the soldiers' surfaces. The delicate balance between preserving the army's integrity and protecting it from further decay became an ongoing struggle.

Modern Techniques in Preservation

Faced with these immense challenges, preservationists turned to modern science for answers. The goal was not just to stop the deterioration but to bring the Terracotta Army as close to its original state as possible. A delicate balance had to be maintained—using technology without overshadowing the craftsmanship of the original artists.

One of the most significant breakthroughs came in the realm of paint preservation. When researchers realized that the traditional methods of preservation were causing more harm than good, they began to explore innovative solutions. Special chemicals were developed to seal the fragile paint before exposure to air. These chemicals, applied in micro-layers, acted as a protective barrier, allowing archaeologists to handle the pieces without fear of losing the vivid colors that gave the soldiers their lifelike appearance. For example, a method known as "PEG impregnation" was used, where polyethylene glycol was applied to the painted surfaces, stabilizing the pigments without altering their natural composition.

Another advancement was the use of 3D scanning and modeling technologies. Before handling or restoring any fragment of a soldier, researchers would create a digital model of the piece using high-resolution scanners. This allowed them to study every crack, break, and missing piece in meticulous detail. With these digital models, restorers could simulate how different parts of a soldier would fit together, reducing the risk of damaging fragile pieces during the physical restoration process. This technology also proved invaluable in reassembling chariots and horses, whose more intricate parts required precision that was impossible to achieve by hand alone.

Climate-controlled storage and exhibition spaces were also critical in preserving the soldiers. Special cases were designed to maintain constant humidity and temperature levels, mimicking the conditions of the underground chambers where the army had lain for centuries. By controlling these variables, restorers could slow down the effects of time, allowing the soldiers to stand on display without risking further degradation.

Ongoing Restoration Projects

Restoration efforts are not a one-time endeavor; they are ongoing projects that require constant attention. As new technologies emerge and more of the mausoleum is uncovered, teams of specialists continue to refine and improve their methods.

One of the most ambitious restoration projects has been the reassembly of the broken warriors. When the army was first discovered, many of the soldiers were found in pieces, scattered across the vaults. It took years of painstaking work to piece together thousands of fragments. Teams of restorers would work like detectives, examining each shard of terracotta for clues about where it might belong. Some soldiers were rebuilt from nearly 50 different pieces. The process required not just technical skill but also patience and an almost artistic intuition.

In some cases, the restoration process led to surprising discoveries. As restorers worked to reassemble one particular soldier, they found a small cavity inside its torso. Further investigation revealed that it was a hidden compartment, likely intended to hold some kind of offering or relic, although the contents had long since disappeared. These kinds of discoveries continue to shed new light on the rituals and beliefs of the Qin Dynasty, adding depth to our understanding of the army's purpose.

Another ongoing project involves the excavation of new sections of the mausoleum. While the Terracotta Army is undoubtedly the most famous part of Qin Shi Huang's tomb, the entire complex is vast and largely unexplored. Archaeologists believe that there are still thousands of warriors, chariots, and horses waiting to be uncovered, each one presenting new challenges in terms of preservation. Excavating these new areas is a slow and careful process, with teams working under strict protocols to ensure that no damage is done to the fragile artifacts.

Restorers also continue to work on preserving the weapons that were buried with the soldiers. Many of the warriors originally held bronze swords, spears, and crossbows, all of which have suffered from corrosion over time. Specialized treatments, including electrochemical methods, are used to remove rust and restore the luster of these ancient weapons. In some cases, new methods are being tested to replicate the ancient techniques used to forge these weapons, allowing researchers to understand the craftsmanship that went into equipping the emperor's army.

Global Contributions to Preservation

The preservation and restoration of the Terracotta Army is not just a Chinese effort—it is a global project that has drawn expertise and resources from around the world. International teams of archaeologists, chemists, engineers, and art historians have collaborated with Chinese scholars to tackle the immense challenges posed by the excavation and preservation of this monumental find.

One of the most significant global contributions came from Germany, where a team of scientists developed a technique for preserving the terracotta soldiers' paint. Using a mixture of nanoparticles, the German researchers were able to create a coating that prevented the paint from peeling off when exposed to air. This collaboration between Chinese and German experts marked a turning point in the preservation efforts, allowing future excavations to proceed without the fear of losing irreplaceable details.

Italy, known for its rich history of preserving ancient art and monuments, has also played a key role. Italian conservators shared their expertise in restoring statues and frescoes, providing valuable insights into how to handle the fragile surfaces of the terracotta warriors. Their experience in dealing with complex restorations—such as the preservation of Pompeii's ancient ruins—proved invaluable in developing new techniques for reassembling and stabilizing the soldiers.

In addition to technical expertise, international funding has been crucial to the ongoing preservation efforts. Organizations like UNESCO have designated the Terracotta Army as a World Heritage Site, providing financial support and raising awareness about the importance of its preservation. This global recognition has helped secure resources for continued research and restoration, ensuring that the Terracotta Army remains a part of humanity's shared cultural heritage.

Finally, international exhibitions have played a pivotal role in raising global awareness about the Terracotta Army. By sending some of the soldiers on tours around the world, China has not only shared its cultural treasure with millions but also generated funds for ongoing preservation efforts. These exhibitions have fostered a deeper appreciation of the Terracotta Army's significance and the need to protect it for future generations.

CHAPTER 8

Visitor Experiences and Stories

As visitors step into the vast halls of the Terracotta Army, they are greeted not just by a remarkable archaeological site, but by a powerful connection to the ancient past. Each figure, meticulously crafted over two millennia ago, stands as a sentinel of history, inviting guests to explore the life, culture, and ambitions of the first Emperor of China, Qin Shi Huang. The experience is transformative; tourists find themselves immersed in an atmosphere where the echoes of the past resonate, igniting a sense of wonder and reverence. Walking among the warriors, one can almost feel the weight of history, as if the very ground is infused with stories waiting to be uncovered.

In this chapter, we delve into the unique experiences and stories shared by those who have journeyed to this iconic site. From the awe-inspiring moment of witnessing the soldiers rise from the earth to the intimate reflections sparked by these ancient figures, visitors leave with memories that linger long after they've returned home. Their encounters range from emotional revelations to whimsical coincidences, illustrating how the Terracotta Army serves as a bridge connecting individuals across cultures and generations. As we explore these stories, we uncover not just the impact of the Terracotta Army on tourism but also its profound ability to inspire reflection on legacy, mortality, and the enduring human spirit.

The Tourist Journey: Walking Among the Warriors

Imagine stepping into a vast underground vault, with rows upon rows of life-sized warriors staring stoically ahead, their expressions frozen in time. You can almost hear the echoes of marching footsteps, feel the silent hum of military discipline, and sense the weight of history surrounding you. For visitors to the site of the Terracotta Army, this experience feels like walking into an ancient world, a tangible connection to the distant past.

The first glimpse of the Terracotta Army is breathtaking. As you walk toward the excavation pits, you are greeted by towering statues of soldiers, each intricately crafted with individual expressions, hairstyles, and postures. The enormity of the site strikes you before anything else. Thousands of warriors stretch out before you in organized formations, as though they are still guarding the tomb of Qin Shi Huang, the first Emperor of China.

For many, the moment is deeply humbling. Standing face-to-face with these silent sentinels, visitors often describe feeling as though they've been transported back to the ancient Qin dynasty. The warriors seem alive in their realism, as though they are waiting for the command to march. It's a striking contrast between life and death—these terracotta figures, crafted over two thousand years ago, stand as a monument to human ambition and creativity.

The experience is immersive, from the minute you walk into the museum complex to the moment you step out, minds reeling from the historical and artistic grandeur. Visitors walk through several pits where ongoing excavations still reveal new finds, creating a dynamic and ever-evolving narrative. There's a sense of exploration, with each visitor feeling they are witnessing a live connection to history. The artifacts are surrounded by a careful balance of modern preservation efforts and ancient craftsmanship, a combination that offers a unique journey through time.

The scale of the site is something that words often fail to capture. Visitors are left in awe not only of the physical size of the army—estimated to number over 8,000 figures—but also of the meticulous detail in every soldier. The warriors, ranging from foot soldiers to archers to chariot drivers, stand in distinct formations, reflecting the real-life structure of Qin Shi Huang's army. It's an overwhelming spectacle, and as visitors walk along the elevated pathways surrounding the pits, they are given the rare opportunity to contemplate this grand military force in all its preserved glory.

Unique Stories and Encounters

Over the years, many visitors have shared unique, almost mystical experiences while visiting the Terracotta Army. Some describe a deep, almost spiritual connection to the site, as though the warriors are watching over them. For others, it's a sense of overwhelming awe at the sheer scale of the project and the realization that they are standing in the midst of one of the world's greatest archaeological discoveries.

One particularly touching story is that of a young historian from Italy, who, after years of studying the Terracotta Army in books and documentaries, finally had the opportunity to visit the site. Upon seeing the warriors in person, she broke down in tears. She later described it as a moment of "meeting her heroes"—not the warriors themselves, but the artists and craftsmen who had dedicated their lives to creating these figures. For her, the trip was more than just a visit to a historical site; it was a journey of personal connection, where she felt she could finally honor the hands that had molded these ancient masterpieces.

Another unforgettable story is of a retired soldier from the United States who visited the site during a global tour of military history landmarks. For him, the Terracotta Army symbolized the eternal vigilance of soldiers throughout history. As he gazed upon the vast rows of warriors, he reflected on his own time in service and the deep camaraderie soldiers feel across time and culture. He later described the visit as one of the most emotional moments of his life, where he felt the weight of shared experiences with those who had served centuries before.

Some visitors even report strange coincidences. One such story comes from a Chinese family who had traveled hundreds of miles to visit the army. As they stood looking at the figures, one of the elderly members of the family pointed out a warrior whose face bore an uncanny resemblance to a long-deceased ancestor. The resemblance was so striking that even the museum guide commented on it, leading the family to joke that their ancestor must have been reincarnated as a terracotta soldier. Although it was likely just a coincidence, the experience left the family feeling as though they had made a personal connection to their nation's past.

Not all stories are quite as mystical, but the shared experiences of wonder, reflection, and discovery are universal. Whether it's a child staring wide-eyed at the soldiers for the first time, or an elderly couple reminiscing about the ancient world, every visitor leaves the Terracotta Army with a unique story to tell.

The Impact on Local and Global Tourism

The discovery of the Terracotta Army in 1974 catapulted Xi'an, the capital of Shaanxi province, onto the world stage as a premier destination for tourists. What was once a relatively unknown region became a global hotspot, attracting millions of visitors from around the world.

The local economy has experienced a massive boom due to this influx of tourists. Hotels, restaurants, and shops have sprung up around the area, catering to the constant flow of visitors. The region has become synonymous with the Terracotta Army, and it is not uncommon to see souvenir shops filled with miniature warriors, chariots, and horses crafted from clay, just like their ancient counterparts. Local artisans have found new ways to keep the ancient craft alive, producing replicas that allow tourists to take a piece of history home with them.

For global tourism, the Terracotta Army has become a bucket-list destination, standing alongside iconic landmarks like the Pyramids of Giza and the Colosseum in Rome. Travelers are drawn not only by the archaeological significance but by the cultural richness of the site. The army represents more than just an ancient burial ground; it's a symbol of China's historical depth and its contributions to the world's heritage.

The sheer number of visitors has led to significant efforts in managing the flow of tourists and preserving the integrity of the site. In recent years, the Chinese government has implemented various preservation measures, ensuring that the army can be enjoyed by future generations without compromising its historical value. These measures include limiting visitor numbers, constructing advanced viewing platforms, and establishing strict protocols for photography and interaction with the exhibits.

Xi'an, once primarily known for its role as the starting point of the ancient Silk Road, has now been rebranded as the city of the Terracotta Warriors. It draws history enthusiasts, tourists, and scholars from all corners of the globe, making it a center for cultural exchange. Museums, both in China and abroad, have hosted traveling exhibitions of the warriors, spreading their historical significance even further. These global exhibitions have piqued the curiosity of millions, encouraging them to make the pilgrimage to the original site in Xi'an.

Visitor Reflections and Memories

After the initial awe subsides and visitors leave the excavation pits, many describe feeling a profound sense of connection to human history. The Terracotta Army serves as a reminder of the lengths to which humanity has gone in its pursuit of immortality, legacy, and power. Visitors often reflect on the timelessness of these desires, noting how, despite vast differences in culture and era, the human need for legacy remains a universal constant.

One particularly memorable visitor reflection came from a Chinese-American woman who visited the site with her two young children. She spoke about the importance of connecting her children with their heritage, describing how seeing the warriors in person allowed them to understand their ancestors' contributions to the world in a way that textbooks never could. She said, "It's one thing to read about it in school, but standing here, seeing these soldiers face to face—it makes history come alive."

For some, the visit prompts deeper philosophical reflections. One traveler, after touring the site, wrote in a blog: "Standing among these warriors, you realize how fleeting life is. The emperor built this grand tomb, surrounded himself with these incredible soldiers to guard him in death. But even he, with all his power and ambition, couldn't escape time. And now, centuries later, we stand here, gazing at his silent army, while he is dust. It's a humbling reminder of our own mortality."

Others reflect on the artistic brilliance of the figures, marveling at how craftsmen from over two millennia ago could create such lifelike and intricate sculptures. For many art enthusiasts, seeing the warriors up close sparks a renewed appreciation for the creative endeavors of ancient civilizations. The detailed facial features, the variations in armor and posture, and the careful attention to realism leave a lasting impression on visitors.

The Terracotta Army leaves no one indifferent. Visitors leave not just with memories of awe-inspiring statues, but with a deep respect for the hands that created them, the emperor they were made for, and the ancient civilization that produced such a monumental legacy. The warriors, once buried and forgotten, have now re-entered the consciousness of the modern world, and for those lucky enough to visit them, they leave an indelible mark on the heart and mind.

CONCLUSION

The Enduring Legacy

As the sun rises over the ancient city of Xi'an, casting its first light on the cavernous pits that house the Terracotta Army, one can't help but feel the weight of history. This is not just an archaeological site—it is a living testament to the ambition of an emperor who wanted to rule forever. More than 2,000 years later, the Terracotta Army stands as a symbol of both ancient China's grandeur and the indelible mark Qin Shi Huang left on the world.

In the modern world, the Terracotta Army has become more than just a symbol of China's past; it has transformed into an international cultural treasure. Tourists from all over the globe walk among the silent warriors, marveling at their craftsmanship, their scale, and the sheer audacity of the project. These figures, frozen in time, have sparked the imaginations of scholars, historians, and visitors alike. The intricacies of each soldier—unique facial expressions, individualized armor—continue to be a source of fascination, as if they could come to life at any moment and tell the stories of their creator.

But the army's significance today stretches beyond tourism or historical interest. It serves as a reminder of how humanity seeks immortality through art, legacy, and monumental achievements. The Terracotta Army is a part of a broader conversation about the lengths civilizations will go to ensure their memory endures. It has become an emblem not just of China's heritage, but of the universal human desire to be remembered.

China itself has embraced this legacy in modern times. The country has dedicated considerable resources to preserving the site and sharing it with the world. Museums and exhibitions across continents have displayed select pieces from the army, drawing in millions of visitors and raising awareness about this ancient wonder. The Terracotta Army has traveled the world, from Paris to New York, inviting people everywhere to explore a piece of China's past. In doing so, the warriors have become cultural ambassadors, representing a proud history that reaches back over two millennia.

Yet the army also serves as a stark reminder of power and ambition. In many ways, the Terracotta Army reflects the tension between creation and destruction, between life and death. Qin Shi Huang sought to achieve immortality, not through philosophy or art, but through sheer force of will. The Terracotta Army, while a work of unparalleled artistic beauty, was also born from the intense labor of thousands of workers, many of whom likely perished in the construction process. It is a monument to both human creativity and the darker side of power.

Today, the Terracotta Army stands as a point of reflection. In a world that constantly changes, it reminds us of the endurance of human craftsmanship, of the dreams of immortality, and of the cost of ambition. The army may be silent, but its presence speaks volumes.

Lessons from History

The Terracotta Army, while rooted in a specific moment in history, offers lessons that transcend time. At its core, it is a story about legacy—about how individuals and societies wish to be remembered. For Qin Shi Huang, the army was a means of ensuring that his reign, his power, and his accomplishments would be eternal. In a way, he succeeded: more than 2,000 years after his death, the world continues to marvel at what he left behind. But this legacy also invites deeper questions about the nature of power and the desire for immortality.

One of the clearest lessons from the Terracotta Army is the complexity of human ambition. Qin Shi Huang was not content with unifying China, a monumental achievement in itself. He wanted to conquer death, to ensure that his rule would extend into eternity. His desire for control over life and the afterlife led to one of the most ambitious projects in human history. The lesson here is not just about ambition, but about the lengths people will go to secure their place in history.

However, the Terracotta Army also teaches us about the unintended consequences of such ambition. The emperor's quest for immortality required immense resources and labor, and it is widely believed that many of the workers who built his mausoleum were buried alive to protect its secrets. This dark aspect of the Terracotta Army serves as a cautionary tale: the pursuit of power and legacy can come at a steep human cost. The grandeur of the Terracotta Army is inextricably linked to the sacrifices made by those who created it.

Another key lesson is about the importance of memory and preservation. The fact that the Terracotta Army remained hidden for over two millennia is a testament to the passage of time and the ways in which history can be lost and rediscovered. The world might never have known about the Terracotta Army had it not been for the chance discovery by farmers in 1974. This serves as a reminder of the fragility of history, and the importance of preserving and protecting cultural heritage. If we do not take steps to care for the legacies of the past, they may be lost forever.

Lastly, the Terracotta Army speaks to the enduring power of art and craftsmanship. Each warrior, horse, and chariot was meticulously crafted by skilled artisans, reflecting the artistic excellence of ancient China. The attention to detail is astonishing—every soldier has a distinct face, posture, and expression. This dedication to individuality within a collective whole speaks to the value of human creativity and the role of art in shaping history. It is a reminder that even in the service of power, art can transcend its original purpose and become something more—a lasting tribute to human ingenuity.

Qin Shi Huang's Vision: Realized or Not?

Did Qin Shi Huang's grand vision for immortality come to fruition? The answer to this question is both complex and paradoxical.

In one sense, Qin Shi Huang's dream of ruling forever was not realized. He did not achieve physical immortality; his body was laid to rest in the vast underground mausoleum, and his dynasty collapsed just a few years after his death. The Qin Dynasty, which he founded, lasted only 15 years—far shorter than the legacy he had hoped to create. His obsession with control and immortality ultimately failed to prevent the inevitable: death came for him as it does for all humans.

However, in another sense, Qin Shi Huang's vision was realized in ways he could not have imagined. The Terracotta Army has ensured that his name and his reign are remembered centuries later. While he did not achieve eternal life in the traditional sense, his legacy has endured. People across the globe know the name Qin Shi Huang, and his Terracotta Army is one of the most famous archaeological discoveries in history. In this way, he did achieve a form of immortality—through his impact on history and the monumental works he left behind.

Moreover, Qin Shi Huang's vision of a unified China has had lasting consequences. Although his dynasty was short-lived, the unification of China under his rule laid the foundation for the future of the Chinese empire. The centralization of power, the standardization of weights, measures, and writing, and the construction of the Great Wall—all these achievements have had a profound and lasting influence on China's development. In this respect, Qin Shi Huang's vision of a strong, unified China was indeed realized, even if not in the way he might have anticipated.

Yet, there remains an irony to Qin Shi Huang's quest for immortality. While his legacy has endured, it is often remembered with a mix of awe and ambivalence. The Terracotta Army stands as a monument to his greatness, but also as a reminder of the human cost of his ambition. His name is remembered, but not always in the glorified manner he might have hoped. He is seen as both a visionary and a tyrant, a man who achieved great things but at a great cost.

Ultimately, Qin Shi Huang's vision was both realized and not realized. He did not conquer death, but he did achieve a lasting place in history. His desire for immortality, while not fulfilled in the way he intended, has been realized in a different form. The Terracotta Army, as his lasting legacy, ensures that his name and his story will continue to be told for generations to come.

As we conclude our journey through the history, significance, and enduring legacy of the Terracotta Army, it becomes clear that this ancient wonder is more than just a collection of clay figures. It is a window into the mind of a man who sought to transcend the boundaries of life and death, a reflection of the complex interplay between power, art, and ambition.

The Terracotta Army stands as a testament to the ingenuity and creativity of ancient China, a civilization that produced wonders on a scale that continues to astound us today. It reminds us of the timeless nature of human ambition—the desire to leave a mark, to be remembered, to outlast the limitations of mortality. Yet, it also serves as a cautionary tale, reminding us of the costs of such ambition and the sacrifices that are often demanded in the pursuit of greatness.

In the modern world, the Terracotta Army continues to inspire awe, curiosity, and reflection. It connects us to a distant past, but its lessons are as relevant today as they were two millennia ago. As we walk among the silent warriors, we are reminded of the enduring power of history and the legacies we leave behind.

In the end, the Terracotta Army is not just Qin Shi Huang's monument—it is a monument to all of humanity. It is a reminder that, while we may not achieve immortality in the literal sense, our actions, our creations, and our legacies can live on long after we are gone.

APPENDICES

Timeline of the Construction and Discovery

- 246 BCE: Construction begins on the mausoleum of Emperor Qin Shi Huang, shortly after he ascends the throne as the king of Qin at the age of 13. Thousands of workers are tasked with building the elaborate tomb and its Terracotta Army, intended to protect the emperor in the afterlife.

- 221 BCE: Qin Shi Huang unifies China, becoming the first emperor of the Qin Dynasty. The construction of the Terracotta Army continues during his reign, reflecting the emperor's immense power and ambition.

- 210 BCE: Qin Shi Huang dies, and his mausoleum, along with the Terracotta Army, is sealed. The exact location of the emperor's tomb remains a secret.

- 1974 CE: Farmers digging a well near Xi'an accidentally uncover fragments of the Terracotta warriors, leading to one of the most significant archaeological discoveries of the 20th century.

- 1976 CE: Full-scale excavation begins, uncovering thousands of life-sized warriors, horses, and chariots, each with unique features.

- 1987 CE: UNESCO designates the Mausoleum of the First Qin Emperor and the Terracotta Army a World Heritage Site, cementing its global cultural significance.

GLOSSARY OF TERMS

1. **Acrobat Figures:** Sculptures found near the Terracotta Army site that depict performers and entertainers. These figures provide insight into the entertainment and cultural practices of the Qin Dynasty, highlighting the emperor's interest in not only military strength but also in the arts.

2. **Afterlife:** A key concept in many ancient cultures, including Qin-era China. The afterlife refers to the belief that life continues in some form after death. Emperor Qin Shi Huang believed that his power and empire would extend into the afterlife, which is why he commissioned the Terracotta Army to protect him after death.

3. **Artisan:** Skilled craftsmen who were responsible for the creation of the Terracotta warriors, their weapons, armor, and the emperor's tomb. These artisans worked in specialized teams, each focusing on different parts of the statues, from sculpting the heads to crafting weapons.

4. **Armor:** The protective gear worn by soldiers in the Terracotta Army. While the original armor was made of metal or leather, the statues themselves were crafted with detailed clay depictions of the

armor, showcasing different styles based on the soldiers' ranks and roles.

5. **Bronze Weaponry:** The Terracotta Army was equipped with various bronze weapons, including swords, spears, and crossbows. Bronze was the primary metal used for weapons in ancient China and demonstrated advanced metallurgical techniques for the time.

6. **Cavalryman:** A member of the cavalry, or horse-mounted soldiers. In the Terracotta Army, cavalrymen are depicted holding reins and guiding their horses, showcasing their role as mobile and swift soldiers capable of flanking enemies.

7. **Chariot:** A two-wheeled horse-drawn vehicle used in ancient warfare for speed, mobility, and battlefield advantage.

8. **Crossbow:** A ranged weapon that was widely used by the Qin army and featured among the weapons found with the Terracotta Army. Crossbows were revolutionary in ancient Chinese warfare, providing greater accuracy and power compared to traditional bows.

9. **Divination:** A practice used in ancient China to predict the future or make important decisions,

often through rituals involving oracle bones or other methods. Emperor Qin Shi Huang was known to consult diviners and believed in supernatural guidance for his reign and afterlife.

10. **Emperor Qin Shi Huang:** The first emperor of China and the ruler who ordered the construction of the Terracotta Army and his massive mausoleum. He unified China in 221 BCE and laid the foundation for the Qin Dynasty, which is remembered for its military strength, centralized government, and cultural contributions.

11. **Excavation:** The process of uncovering historical artifacts and remains from beneath the ground, often done by archaeologists. The excavation of the Terracotta Army site began in 1974 and continues to this day, revealing new treasures and information about Qin Dynasty China.

12. **Infantryman:** A foot soldier in the Terracotta Army, representing the bulk of the emperor's forces. These soldiers were arranged in battle formation, standing at the front lines with various weapons like spears, swords, and shields.

13. **Lacquer:** A protective coating made from tree sap that was used to coat the Terracotta warriors and their weapons. Over time, the lacquer has

deteriorated, but originally, it would have given the warriors a vibrant and polished appearance.

14. **Li Si:** The chief advisor to Emperor Qin Shi Huang and a major figure in the Qin government. Li Si was instrumental in many of the emperor's policies, including the standardization of currency, weights, measures, and the creation of the Great Wall of China.

15. **Mausoleum:** A grand tomb or burial place, often for royalty or individuals of great importance. Emperor Qin Shi Huang's mausoleum, located near Xi'an, is one of the largest and most elaborate tombs ever constructed, and it houses the Terracotta Army.

16. **Mandate of Heaven:** An ancient Chinese belief that heaven granted emperors the right to rule based on their ability to govern well and fairly. Qin Shi Huang claimed this divine authority, which justified his rule over China.

17. **Pit 1:** The largest of the three main excavation sites at the Terracotta Army complex, containing over 6,000 life-sized warriors arranged in battle formation. It is believed to represent the core of the emperor's army, with infantry soldiers, archers, and chariots.

18. **Pit 2:** The second-largest pit, featuring more specialized units, including cavalry, archers, and war chariots. This pit demonstrates the diverse military strategies employed by the Qin army.

19. **Pit 3:** The smallest pit, often referred to as the command center of the Terracotta Army. It contains high-ranking officers and chariots, believed to represent the generals who would have overseen the army in both life and the afterlife.

20. **Qin Dynasty:** The first imperial dynasty of China, lasting from 221 to 206 BCE. It was founded by Qin Shi Huang and is known for unifying China, establishing a centralized government, and beginning massive infrastructure projects like the Great Wall and the Terracotta Army.

21. **Terracotta:** A type of clay used in pottery, sculpture, and architectural decoration, known for its reddish-brown color.

22. **Tomb Complex:** The entire burial site of Emperor Qin Shi Huang, including the central mausoleum, the surrounding pits containing the Terracotta Army, and other yet-to-be-excavated sections. This complex is believed to be vast, with many sections still undiscovered.

23. **UNESCO World Heritage Site:** A designation given to cultural or natural sites of outstanding universal value. The Terracotta Army and the Mausoleum of the First Qin Emperor were designated as a UNESCO World Heritage Site in 1987 due to their historical significance and preservation of ancient Chinese culture.

24. **Vassal States:** Smaller regions or kingdoms that were under the control of the Qin state before its unification of China. Many of the soldiers in the Terracotta Army likely represent warriors from these various states that Qin Shi Huang conquered during his reign.

25. **War Chariot:** A two-wheeled, horse-drawn vehicle used by soldiers in ancient Chinese warfare. In the Terracotta Army, chariots are depicted alongside soldiers, reflecting the importance of mobility and battlefield strategy in the Qin military.